W9-ACJ-148

CROSSWORD AMERICA

THE 50 STATES

Written by Cathryn J. Long

Illustrated by Larry Nolte

LOWELL HOUSE JUVENILE

LOS ANGELES

NTC/Contemporary Publishing Group

Published by Lowell House
A division of NTC/Contemporary Publishing Group, Inc.
4255 West Touhy Avenue, Lincolnwood (Chicago), Illinois 60646-1975 U.S.A.

Managing Director and Publisher: Jack Artenstein
Director of Publishing Services: Rena Copperman
Editorial Director: Brenda Pope-Ostrow
Editor: Joanna Siebert
Designer: Carolyn Wendt
Cover Designer: Kristi Mathias

Lowell House books can be purchased at special discounts
when ordered in bulk for premiums and special sales.
Contact Customer Service at the above address,
or call 1-800-323-4900.

Printed and bound in the United States of America

Library of Congress Catalog Card Number: 98-75615

ISBN: 0-7373-0173-2

10 9 8 7 6 5 4 3 2 1

CONTENTS

To the Teacher and Parent

The crossword puzzles in this book are a practical and fun review of U.S. history and geography. These puzzles teach important facts about the states. They provide an alternative way of learning that reinforces textbook work. Students can do the puzzles individually or in small groups. Because the puzzles emphasize reading comprehension, vocabulary, and spelling, they have a place in language arts teaching, too. Parents, other home teachers, and teachers of English as a Second Language will also find the puzzles useful.

Each puzzle focuses on one to three states, with an emphasis on geography and how people live in each state today. Capital cities and important historic sites are mentioned throughout. To find the clues and complete each puzzle, students will need to *read and understand* the introductory paragraphs, as well as *locate information in illustrations or maps* that accompany each puzzle. Students can also *locate an appropriate word on the alphabetical list of words* provided with each puzzle as another aid in solving the puzzle. They may need to *refer to the map* provided on page 5 for some clues. If your students are unfamiliar with this type of puzzle, review with them the word numbering system and the way "across" words give clues for "down" words, and vice versa.

If you have already taught about the state (or states) that is featured for a puzzle, you may want to challenge students to complete as much of the puzzle as they can without reading the introduction, looking at the illustrations, or using the word list.

For the Puzzle Player

Did you know that ice-cream cones were first served in Missouri? Or that Minnesota has more lakes than any other state (over 10,000!)? Have you heard that Alaska is called the Last Frontier? This book will help you review these and many other facts about the states by solving crossword puzzles. All the clues you need to solve each puzzle are included with it. There are four ways to find clues:

1. Read the topic summary.
2. Look carefully at the pictures or maps that go with the puzzle.
3. Look for the right word in the puzzle word list.
4. Refer to the map on this page.

The puzzles in this book focus on one to three states. You can find each state on the map below. Solve each puzzle in any order you wish. Have fun learning about this amazing country in *Crossword America*!

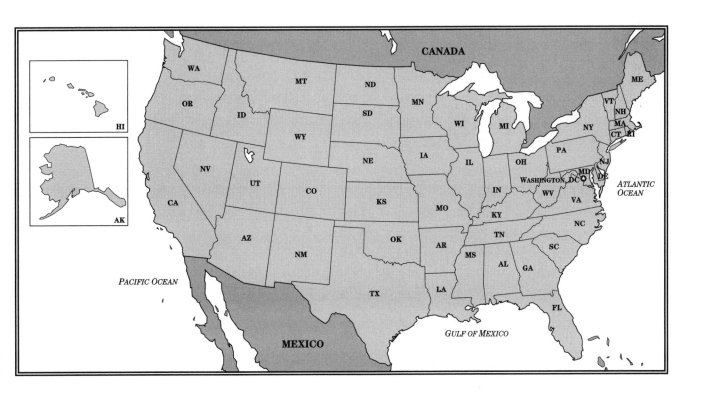

HAWAII

A loha! That expression means "love" in Hawaiian, and it is used to say "hello" and "good-bye." The state of Hawaii is a group of islands located in the middle of the north Pacific Ocean. Many of the islands are so small that no one lives on them permanently.

The Hawaiian Islands were first settled by Polynesian people who traveled there from other Pacific islands. Before becoming a state, the islands had several kinds of governments. For over a hundred years, Polynesian monarchs ruled. Today, you can visit some of the palaces where they once lived. The last monarch, Queen Liliuokalani, was the author of a favorite Hawaiian song, "Aloha Oe" or "Farewell to Thee." In 1893, Hawaii became a republic with elected leaders. It was made a United States territory in 1900. In 1959, Hawaii became the fiftieth state.

Hawaii produces tropical crops, especially pineapples, sugar, and coffee. However, its biggest industry is tourism. People come for the warm air, the clean beaches, the beautiful landscape, and the good shopping. Like the visitors, Hawaii's people come from all over the world. No ethnic group is in the majority there.

The Hawaiian island with the biggest population is Oahu, where the capital, Honolulu, is located. Near Honolulu is Pearl Harbor. A Japanese attack on the U.S. naval base there threw the United States into World War II.

The island of Hawaii is often called the Big Island because it is the largest in the state. There, at Hawaii Volcanoes National Park, you may be able to see active volcanoes spewing lava, superhot liquid rock from deep underground. In fact, all the state's islands were formed by cooled lava that turned into land. Popular tourist attractions on the island of Kauai include Mount Waialeale, which has the most rainy days on earth, and Waimea Canyon.

Across

4. Hawaii has this rank among states, according to when they were admitted to the union.
7. No ethnic group in Hawaii can claim to be this.
8. Hawaii was one just before it became a state.
9. Capital of Hawaii
11. Name of the harbor attacked by Japan that caused the United States to enter World War II
13. The most populated island in the state of Hawaii
14. Hawaiian greeting
15. Hawaii lies in the middle of the north Pacific _____.
16. Nickname for the island of Hawaii: the ___ Island

Down

1. Temperature of Hawaiian air
2. Name of Hawaii's last queen
3. Mount Waialeale is the most ___ spot in the world.
5. Hawaii is famous for this fruit.
6. Hawaii's largest industry
8. The ones on Mauna Kea are the largest in the world.
10. Volcanic material that originally formed the islands
12. Hawaiian royalty lived in these.

HI Hibiscus

ALASKA

Alaska lies at the northwest tip of North America. It is separated from the main body of the United States by part of Canada. The state is so far north that much of it is continually covered with snow and ice. Yet Alaska is an enormously valuable state.

In the mid-1800s, Russia and the United States both wanted Alaska because of its position as a gateway between Asia and America—plus its valuable fur trade. After the United States bought Alaska from Russia, gold was discovered. This discovery led to a gold rush and the founding of Juneau, which is now Alaska's capital. Alaska became a state just before Hawaii, in 1959. Nine years later, the most valuable resource of all was found at Prudhoe Bay, on the shore of the Arctic Ocean: oil. Today, oil is Alaska's greatest export. During the 1970s, people poured into the state to work in the new oil business. While the oil business still employs many Alaskans, the flood of new jobs has stopped.

Life in Alaska is ruled in many ways by the cold and rugged terrain. Although southern Alaska warms enough to grow crops in summer, most of the state is full of glaciers, ice fields, and mountains. The highest peak in the United States, Mount McKinley, is in the Alaska Range. Although Alaska is about twice the size of Texas, it has a very small population. Alaska is often called the Last Frontier because so much of the land remains unsettled. Roads and railroads are used in Alaska, but boats and airplanes often reach towns more easily.

About 15 percent of Alaskans are Native Americans. Many important Native American traditions are still practiced, such as building temporary snow huts, or igloos, when on hunting trips. Their traditional dogsled travel has become a sport for all Alaskans. One of the most famous sled dog race champions is Susan Butcher. She helps organize the Iditarod race from Anchorage to Nome.

Across

2. Moving masses of ice; there are many in Alaska
4. Name of Alaska's most famous sled dog race
8. Temporary round hut made of snow blocks
10. The export of oil has earned this for Alaskan citizens.
11. Country from which the United States bought Alaska
14. Alaska is about twice as big as this state.
15. Last name of a sled dog race champion
16. Alaskans use these often for travel.
17. Country that lies between Alaska and the lower forty-eight states

Down

1. Name of the bay where oil was first discovered in Alaska
2. Mineral resource that caused a rush to Alaska
3. First valuable product taken from Alaska
5. Form of transportation first used by Native Americans in Alaska and northern Canada
6. Percentage of Alaskans who are Native Americans
7. McKinley is the tallest _____ in the United States.
9. Alaska's most valuable export
12. Capital of Alaska
13. Name of the star that appears along with the Big Dipper on the Alaskan flag

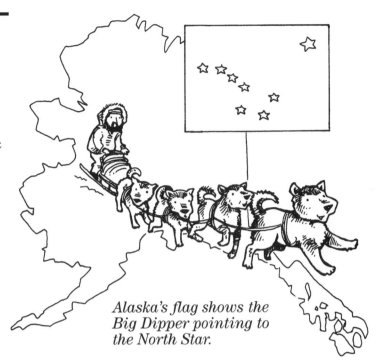

Alaska's flag shows the Big Dipper pointing to the North Star.

Word List

airplanes	dogsled	gold	mountain	Prudhoe
Butcher	fifteen	Iditarod	North	Russia
Canada	fur	igloo	oil	Texas
	glaciers	Juneau	profit	

CALIFORNIA

California, here I come! That's what many people have said since 1848. Beginning with the discovery of gold in that year, newcomers from all over the United States and the world have made the Golden State their home. Today, California has the largest population of all the states in the union. Over 25 percent of Californians are Hispanic, and nearly 10 percent are Asian. California has acted as a gateway to the United States for these people or their ancestors. It is located northwest of Mexico and the rest of Spanish-speaking Central and South America, and east of Asia, which is across the Pacific.

You can find almost every kind of landscape in California. The state's long coast on the Pacific Ocean includes foggy redwood groves in the north and expansive, sunny beaches in the south. The Coast Ranges and the tall Sierra Nevada run through the state from north to south. Between these mountain ranges lies the warm, fertile Central Valley.

People may come to California because of its beauty, but they often stay because of the state's great resources. The cities of San Francisco and Sacramento, now the state capital, grew during the gold rush. However, settlers soon found that the state's real treasure lay in the soil of the Central Valley. The fruits and vegetables that grow there year-round are sold throughout the nation. The huge Los Angeles metropolitan area is best known for Hollywood, where many American movies and television shows are made. Since the 1970s, another part of California has been in the spotlight: Silicon Valley, the area around the city of San Jose. Many computer companies are based there and have brought big changes to businesses and homes worldwide.

Californians do face one serious worry: the danger of earthquakes. But the threat of earthquakes is not enough to keep people from enjoying the unique California lifestyle.

Across

1. A shaking of the ground; a danger in California
5. Continent where one in ten Californians or their ancestors were born
7. Capital of California
9. Movie capital of the United States
12. Name of ranges of California hills and mountains near the sea
15. City that grew during the gold rush: San _____
16. California has more of these than any other state.
17. One of California's most valuable natural resources today
18. Name of the valley where most fruits and vegetables grow in California

Down

California's lovely lands inspired the great naturalist John Muir to argue for the creation of national parks in California. Today, Yosemite is one of California's eight national parks.

2. Tree that grows along the foggy northern California coast
3. Fraction of California's population that is Hispanic
4. Resource that first brought many people to California
6. Name given to the valley where many computer makers work
8. Country bordering California to the southeast
10. Two-letter abbreviation for California
11. Last name of the California naturalist who wanted a national park system
13. California's tallest mountains: the _____ Nevada range
14. San _____ is the city at the center of Silicon Valley.

CA Golden poppy

Word List

Asia	Coast	Hollywood	people	Sierra
CA	earthquake	Jose	quarter	Silicon
Central	Francisco	Mexico	redwood	soil
	gold	Muir	Sacramento	

WASHINGTON AND OREGON

The beautiful volcanic Cascade Range runs through both Washington and Oregon from south to north. In 1980, Mount St. Helens in Washington erupted with huge clouds of smoke and soot, destroying houses and setting off mudslides. Most of the time, though, life is safe in the Pacific Northwest, and many people enjoy hiking and skiing on the tall mountains.

To the west of the Cascades, fertile valleys and a hilly coast get plenty of rain to water fruit and other crops. So much rain falls on Washington's Olympic Peninsula that an unusual rain forest grows there. Trees are so plentiful that Washington is called the Evergreen State, and Oregon leads the nation in producing lumber. East of the Cascades lies a high plateau where the climate is dry and temperatures are much higher in summer and lower in winter.

Between the two states flows the Columbia River. The Columbia once formed the last part of the Oregon Trail, which brought Western settlers to both states. Portland, the largest city in Oregon, lies at the mouth of the Columbia. Citizens of Portland have passed laws to ring their city with a "green belt" of parks in order to slow down the rapid spread of suburbs. Their goal is to make the central city a more attractive place to live and work, while saving farms and wildlands.

Oregonians are known for their concern for the environment—and for bringing government close to the people. In the early 1900s, they passed laws called the Oregon System that became a model for other states. The system included voting rights for women, more direct elections, and the right of citizens to vote directly on issues.

More people live in Washington than in Oregon, and many of those live in or near the Pacific Northwest's largest city, Seattle. In the Seattle area, aerospace and computer software industries are strong. The most famous person in Washington may be Bill Gates, the founder of the giant software company Microsoft.

Across

3. Volcanic chain of mountains in Washington and Oregon
7. Washington peninsula where a rain forest is located
8. Under the Oregon System, a woman could be a _____, just as a man could.
9. Vegetables and _____ grow in the fertile valleys of Washington and Oregon.
10. Oregon produces more of this than any other state.
12. Largest city in Oregon
14. Largest city in Washington
15. People do this on the snowy mountaintops of Washington and Oregon.
16. Name for Washington and Oregon: the Pacific _____

Down

1. Landform east of the Cascade Range
2. People saw Mount St. Helens do this in 1980.
3. River that helps form the border between Washington and Oregon
4. Clouds of smoke and _____ poured from Mount St. Helens when it erupted.
5. Name given to election reforms in Oregon: the Oregon _____
6. Nickname for Washington: the _____ State
7. Name of the trail many settlers followed to Oregon and Washington
11. Last name of the head of Seattle's Microsoft Corporation
13. To stop urban sprawl, Portland has a green _____ of parks around it.

Mount Rainier in Washington

Seattle, Washington, is one of the most popular cities in the United States.

OR *Oregon grape*

WA *Rhododendron*

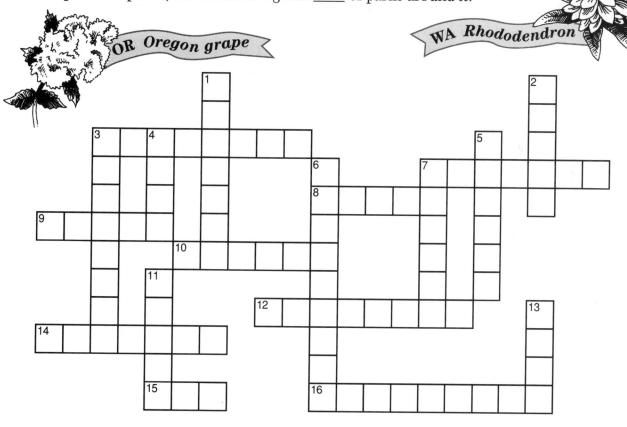

Word List

belt	erupt	lumber	plateau	soot
Cascades	Evergreen	Northwest	Portland	System
Columbia	fruit	Olympic	Seattle	voter
	Gates	Oregon	ski	

NEVADA AND UTAH

Nevada and Utah lie next to each other between the Sierra Nevada, on Nevada's western edge, and the Rocky Mountains, which take up the eastern half of Utah. Both states are high in altitude and have very dry, or arid, climates. The two states share an area called the Great Basin. This rocky, nearly treeless area is surrounded by mountains, but instead of a flat floor, it has ripples of ridges with valleys called "basins" between them. Streams from the mountains flow into the Great Basin only to disappear by evaporating or sinking. In northern Utah, the Great Salt Lake is all that remains of an ancient inland sea. To the south, rivers have carved the land into deep canyons and fantastical shapes.

These lands were not easy to settle, but many people settled in Nevada because of the Comstock Lode, a network of underground veins of gold and silver. That gold and silver helped the Union pay for the Civil War. The Comstock Lode was used up by the early 1900s, leaving ghost towns like Virginia City, which visitors can see today.

Utah was settled by Mormons. This religious group, led by Brigham Young, founded Salt Lake City, Utah's capital, on the edge of the Great Salt Lake. Utah remains about two-thirds Mormon. The headquarters of the church is an important place where many Americans can trace their family records. The Mormon Tabernacle Choir is also world famous.

The people of Nevada and Utah have found ways to make a living in their harsh environment. Dams and irrigation have helped make farming and industry easier, especially in Utah. Tourists also come to Utah for winter skiing and for sight-seeing in the canyon country of the south, where five national parks welcome visitors. Gambling is legal in Nevada. The casinos at Reno and Las Vegas, the two largest cities in Nevada, draw customers from all over the United States. Nevada's capital, Carson City, is, however, a small city.

Across

3. Chief Mormon church, where a famous choir sings
6. Last name of the Mormon leader who founded Salt Lake City
8. Restored historic mining town in Nevada open to visitors: _____ City
10. This attracts many tourists to Nevada.
12. Name of the old gold and silver source, or lode, in Nevada
13. Initials of the large lake in northern Utah
15. Name of the mountains that run through Utah
16. Capital of Nevada: _____ City
17. Nevada's silver and gold helped pay for this war.

Down

Devil's Garden in Arches National Park is one of the many unusual stone formations that can be found in Utah.

1. There are five of this kind of park in southern Utah.
2. Way to spread water to dry farmland; important to Utah and Nevada
4. Term for dry
5. Two-thirds of Utah people claim to be this.
7. Las _____, one of Nevada's major cities built on the business of gambling
9. Winter sport that tourists enjoy in the Utah mountains
11. The Great _____ is a land feature shared by Utah and Nevada.
12. Steep valleys carved by rivers; there are many in southern Utah
14. At the Mormon church headquarters, people can look up this kind of historical record.

UT *Sego lily*

NV *Sagebrush*

Word List

arid	Carson	GSL	national	Vegas
Basin	Civil	gambling	Rocky	Virginia
canyons	Comstock	irrigation	skiing	Young
	family	Mormon	Tabernacle	

IDAHO AND MONTANA

The Rocky Mountains rise high in the states of Idaho and Montana. The Continental Divide runs along the southern part of the border between the two states. There, you can tell if you are in Idaho if the streams run toward the west. If the streams are running eastward, you must be in Montana!

The mountains and foothills have yielded underground treasures in both states. Silver is especially plentiful in Idaho, home of the silver mine at Coeur d'Alene. Both gold and silver were found in Montana, though today, copper, zinc, and oil are among the most profitable minerals. Above ground, the mountains provide lumber and great slopes for skiing. Sun Valley, Idaho, is one of the area's famous winter resorts. In Glacier National Park in northern Montana, you can see beautiful views of the Rocky Mountains.

The land flattens out to the west in Idaho and to the east in Montana. The valley of Idaho's Snake River has proved perfect for the state's most famous crop: potatoes. Montana's high plains produce large crops of wheat. Farmers came to these states in large numbers when the Great Northern Railroad made easy transportation possible. Montana became a state in 1889, and Idaho became one in 1890. Although these states are two of the nation's largest, their populations are among the smallest. Their capitals—Boise, Idaho, and Helena, Montana—are small cities.

Thousands of people in both states belong to Native American tribes, and many live on large reservations there. The Native American heritage of the region is rich. It includes such famous figures as Sacajawea, who helped guide Lewis and Clark across the Rockies, and Chief Joseph, one of the last great leaders of the Nez Percé.

Across

2. Name of a national park in northern Montana
4. Capital of Idaho
5. Line in the Rocky Mountains that determines which way rivers flow: the Continental _____
7. Forest product of Idaho and Montana
10. This crop grows well in former Montana prairie, the high plains.
11. Opposite of large; what populations of Idaho and Montana are
12. Idaho's most famous vegetable
13. Name of the railroad that made Idaho and Montana easier to settle: the Great _____
14. First word in the name of the Idaho city where a large silver mine is located

Down

WELL, IT'S ALL DOWNHILL FROM HERE.

CONTINENTAL DIVIDE

1. Valuable mineral found in both Idaho and Montana
2. Sacajawea acted as one for the Lewis and Clark expedition.
3. Area set aside for a Native American group; there are several in Idaho and Montana
4. Animal that used to roam on the high prairies

6. Name of an Idaho valley with a famous winter resort
8. Idaho river surrounded by potato farms
9. Capital of Montana
12. The Nez _____ are a Native American tribe; Chief Joseph was once their tribal leader.
15. Montana mineral used for fuel

Buffalo once grew fat on prairie grass in Montana's high plains.

ID Syringa

MT Bitterroot

Word List

Boise	Divide	lumber	potato	Snake
buffalo	Glacier	Northern	reservation	Sun
Coeur	guide	oil	silver	wheat
	Helena	Percé	small	

WYOMING AND COLORADO

Colorado has the highest average altitude in the Union, and Wyoming has the second highest. As in other Rocky Mountain states, mining is an important industry. So is recreation. Wyoming includes the oldest American national park, Yellowstone. (A little of the park also falls in Montana and Idaho.) Some early pioneers passing through the region thought they must be near hell, because of Yellowstone's hot springs and geysers. Beautiful mountain scenery and good skiing can be had at many other parks and resorts, such as in Jackson, Wyoming, and Aspen, Colorado.

Although the two states may seem similar, there are important differences. Wyoming has far fewer people: The population of Denver, Colorado, alone is greater than that of the whole state of Wyoming. On Wyoming's high, dry eastern plains that reach to the Rockies, ranching has long been a major way of life. It is said that there are two cows to every citizen in the state. Wyoming is also famous as the Equality State, because women in Wyoming Territory were the first in America to be allowed to vote, hold public office, and serve on juries. In the capital, Cheyenne, most people know the name of Esther Hobart Morris, a leader in the equality movement.

Denver, the capital of Colorado, is the business and cultural center for all the Rocky Mountain region. One of the costs of Denver's continuing growth is smog. Even though the city sits at an altitude of a mile above sea level, the air is often polluted. Colorado Springs is another fast-growing city. It is home to the U.S. Air Force Academy and North American Aerospace Defense Command (NORAD). In the southwestern corner of Colorado, at Mesa Verde National Park, you can see the ancient cliff dwellings of the Anasazi, a Native American people who built with great skill.

Across

2. ____ River, the large Native American reservation in central Wyoming
5. Tribe living in Wyoming today
7. Initials of a person who sought equality for women in Wyoming Territory
9. Name of America's oldest national park, located in Wyoming
11. Short name for the North American Aerospace Defense Command, headquartered in Colorado Springs
13. Denver suffers from this air problem.
15. Colorado town famous as a ski resort
16. Name of the ancient Native American people who built cliff dwellings
18. Wyoming Territory was the first to allow women to do this.

Down

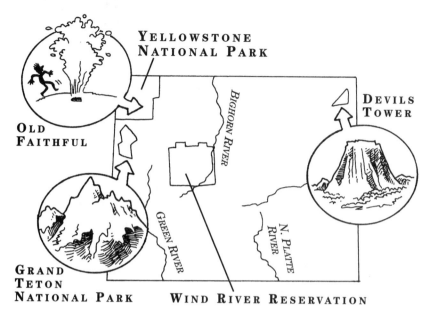

YELLOWSTONE NATIONAL PARK

OLD FAITHFUL

DEVILS TOWER

BIGHORN RIVER

GREEN RIVER

N. PLATTE RIVER

GRAND TETON NATIONAL PARK

WIND RIVER RESERVATION

Wyoming's Wind River Reservation, almost as big as Yellowstone, is home to Shoshone and Arapaho people.

1. Denver's altitude is as high as this.
3. Capital of Wyoming
4. Colorado national park where cliff dwellings are preserved: _____ Verde
6. Some early travelers seeing Yellowstone's hot pools and springs thought they must be near this place.
8. State with the highest average elevation in the United States
10. Nickname for Wyoming: the _____ State
12. Capital of Colorado
14. Home for cows; common in Wyoming
17. The U.S. _____ Force has an academy at Colorado Springs.

CO *Rocky Mountain columbine*

WY *Indian paintbrush*

Word List

Air	Cheyenne	Equality	NORAD	vote
Anasazi	Colorado	hell	pollution	Wind
Aspen	Denver	Mesa	ranch	Yellowstone
	EHM	mile	Shoshone	

19

ARIZONA AND NEW MEXICO

Arizona and New Mexico are located next to each other in the southwestern area of the United States. They share their southern borders with Mexico. In both states, you can find parts of the Rocky Mountains, high plains, and plateaus. In southwestern Arizona, the land dips lower into the Sonoran Desert.

People from nearly every Native American tribe on the continent come to New Mexico every year for the Intertribal Indian Ceremonial. New Mexico is a natural place for the gathering because this state and its neighbor, Arizona, include more than half the reservation land in the United States. At places like Chaco Canyon, New Mexico, you can still visit buildings created by native people hundreds of years before the arrival of Europeans. Today, many tribes continue traditions such as the Pueblo practice of building apartment-style structures of adobe bricks (made from clay mud mixed with straw). The Navajo reservation, located in northeast Arizona and part of New Mexico, is home to the nation's largest tribe. The Navajo raise sheep and farm. They practice traditional crafts including silversmithing and weaving. Discoveries of minerals on Navajo land have helped increase the tribe's income.

A significant part of the population in both states is of Mexican or Spanish heritage. The Spanish language and customs of both groups are an important part of life in cities like Santa Fe, the capital of New Mexico.

People come to Arizona and New Mexico for the dry, healthy air, and to find jobs in the growing economy of these and other warm-climate states in what is known as the Sun Belt. Arizona has had the most growth of the two states, especially in its two largest cities, Tucson and Phoenix, the capital. The natural beauty of the region is another draw. In northern Arizona, the Colorado River has carved out the spectacular Grand Canyon. Blooming deserts and New Mexico's Carlsbad Caverns present other kinds of beauty.

Across

3. Name of a New Mexico canyon with ancient Native American buildings
4. Nickname for the sunny region that includes New Mexico and Arizona
5. Language, other than English, that is an important part of culture in New Mexico and Arizona
11. First word of the name of the Native American ceremonial held yearly in New Mexico
12. Country bordering Arizona and New Mexico to the south
13. Quality of the air in Arizona and New Mexico
14. Tribe famous for building adobe housing
16. Largest Native American tribe in the United States
17. Second word in the name of New Mexico's capital

Down

1. New Mexico city that artist Georgia O'Keeffe helped make into an art center
2. Capital of Arizona
3. Name of famous caverns in New Mexico
6. The Sun Belt state with one of the fastest-growing populations in the nation
7. Animal raised by Navajo ranchers
8. Name of the canyon formed by the Colorado River
9. Two-letter abbreviation for New Mexico
10. Name of the desert in southwest Arizona
15. More than this fraction of U.S. reservation land is in Arizona and New Mexico.

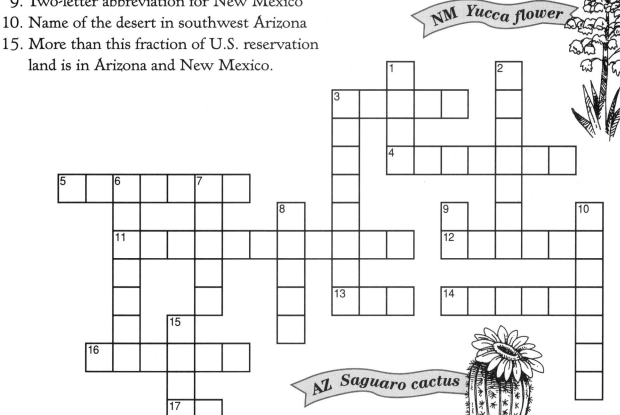

Photo by John Candelario, Courtesy of Museum of New Mexico, Neg. No. 165660

The famous artist Georgia O'Keeffe captured the desert landscape of cities such as Taos, New Mexico.

Photo by John Candelario, Courtesy of Museum of New Mexico, Neg. No. 165657

Georgia O'Keeffe's Ghost Ranch House in New Mexico

NM *Yucca flower*

AZ *Saguaro cactus*

Word List

Arizona	dry	Intertribal	Phoenix	Spanish
Carlsbad	Fe	Mexico	Pueblo	Sun Belt
Chaco	Grand	Navajo	sheep	Taos
	half	NM	Sonoran	

TEXAS AND OKLAHOMA

exas is bigger in area than any state except Alaska. Once, when Texas was part of Mexico, little moved on the vast plains that make up most of the state except cattle. Then American settlers rebelled to form their own "Lone Star" republic, and soon after, in 1845, joined the United States. People poured in to plant cotton (still the leading crop today) and to raise even more cattle. Then, in 1901, Texas's first big oil well, called Spindletop, began producing at a record rate.

Population has grown to suit the size and riches of the state. Texas is second in population only to California. Houston is the biggest city, located near the Gulf of Mexico. There, cotton is processed in mills and oil is processed in refineries and chemical plants for easy shipping. Houston is also famous for its big, covered Astrodome stadium and for its space center. "Hello, Houston" has become a familiar phrase from astronauts on space missions. Dallas, in central Texas, serves as a center for finance and business all over the Southwest. Texas's many other cities include Austin, the capital.

Just north of Texas, the state of Oklahoma is also home to many cattle ranches and oil wells. Tulsa, Oklahoma, is sometimes called "the oil capital of the world." The capital, Oklahoma City, attracted attention worldwide when its federal building was bombed in 1995.

Oklahoma has a special history. In the 1830s, the region was set aside by the U.S. government for Native Americans. Many tribes were forced to move to this "Indian Territory." There, the tribes set up their own forms of government. After the United States refused to accept the Indian area as a state, tribal leaders joined with white settlers to enter the Union. Today, over sixty tribes remain in the state.

Across

1. The Lyndon B. Johnson _____ Center in Houston sends off spacecraft and communicates with astronauts.
4. The rank of Texas among the states in size and population
6. Plants where oil is processed; there are several in Houston
9. Name of the covered sports stadium in Houston
11. More tribes than this multiple of ten live in Oklahoma.
12. The nickname for Texas is the Lone _____ State.
13. Texas's biggest city
15. Initials of the capital of Oklahoma
16. Valuable underground resource in both Texas and Oklahoma

Down

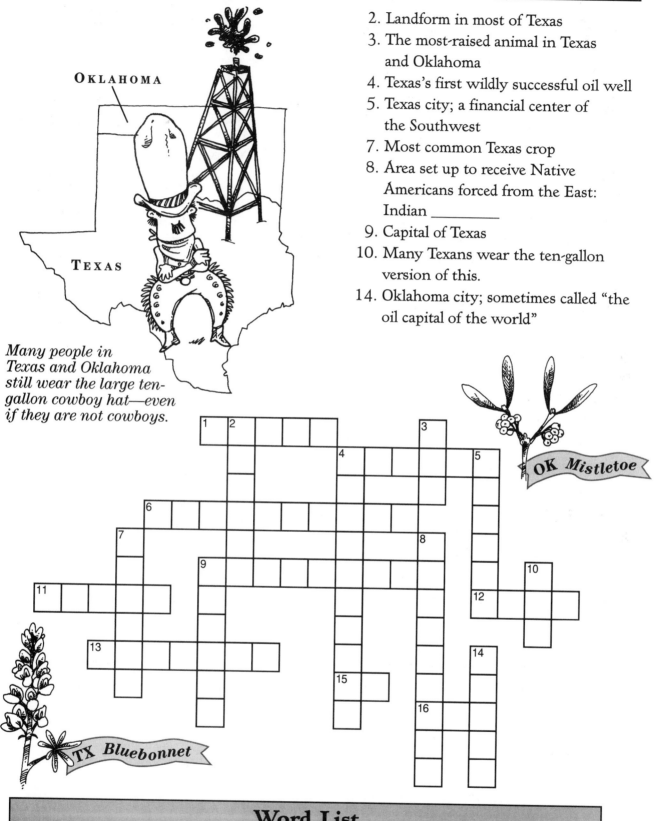

2. Landform in most of Texas
3. The most-raised animal in Texas and Oklahoma
4. Texas's first wildly successful oil well
5. Texas city; a financial center of the Southwest
7. Most common Texas crop
8. Area set up to receive Native Americans forced from the East: Indian _____
9. Capital of Texas
10. Many Texans wear the ten-gallon version of this.
14. Oklahoma city; sometimes called "the oil capital of the world"

OKLAHOMA

TEXAS

Many people in Texas and Oklahoma still wear the large ten-gallon cowboy hat—even if they are not cowboys.

OK Mistletoe

TX Bluebonnet

Word List

Astrodome	cow	OC	second	Star
Austin	Dallas	oil	sixty	Territory
cotton	hat	plains	Space	Tulsa
	Houston	refineries	Spindletop	

NORTH DAKOTA AND SOUTH DAKOTA

Some of the greatest and saddest moments in Native American history took place in the land of the Dakota, also called the Sioux. In 1874, General George Custer discovered gold on Sioux land in the Black Hills (now South Dakota). The Sioux fought the army over that land and, at the Battle of the Little Bighorn, defeated Custer and his men. Later, however, the Sioux leader Crazy Horse was killed and the government took over the Black Hills.

Sioux and other tribes still live in the Dakotas. In 1973, a group called the American Indian Movement gained publicity for Native American rights when they took over the South Dakota Sioux village of Wounded Knee. It was at Wounded Knee that the U.S. Army killed a group of Sioux men, women, and children to end resistance in 1890.

The coming of the railroad and the Homestead Act, which offered free government land, brought settlers to Dakota Territory to farm. They found the vast Great Plains, varied only by oddly shaped, eroded hills called the Badlands in the west and the Black Hills in the southwest. Today, farming and ranching remain major ways of making a living. Wheat is the chief crop in North Dakota, as is corn in South Dakota. In North Dakota, the Garrison Dam on the Missouri River has opened many thousands of acres for farming.

Oil and minerals have also been found in both Dakotas, and gold is still being taken from the Black Hills. In fact, that is the location of the largest American gold mine, the Homestake Mine. Also in the Black Hills is Mount Rushmore, a mountain carved with huge stone portraits of George Washington, Thomas Jefferson, Theodore Roosevelt, and Abraham Lincoln.

Cities in the Dakotas are not large. The captials of both states—Bismarck, North Dakota, and Pierre, South Dakota—were once trading posts on the Missouri River.

Across

1. Precious metal found in the Black Hills by General Custer
4. Biggest crop in South Dakota
5. The capitals of both North and South Dakota are on this river.
6. Name of the South Dakota hills where Mount Rushmore is located
8. Name of the large gold mine in South Dakota
9. Name of the mountain on which the faces of four presidents are carved
12. _____ Knee, a famous Sioux village
14. Main crop in North Dakota
15. Another name for the Sioux

Sculptors have been carving a memorial to Crazy Horse on a mountain in the Black Hills since 1948. When finished, it will be the largest sculpture in the world.

Down

1. North Dakota dam on the Missouri that has allowed more farming
2. The act that provided free government land to farmers
3. The general who made a last stand at the Little Bighorn
6. Capital of North Dakota
7. Initials of the group that took over Wounded Knee to gain publicity for Native American rights
10. Second word in the name of the Sioux leader represented in a mountain-sized statue being carved in South Dakota
11. Initials of the state for which Pierre is the capital
13. Oddly eroded hills in the Dakotas are called the ___lands.
16. Initials of the Roosevelt whose face appears on Mount Rushmore

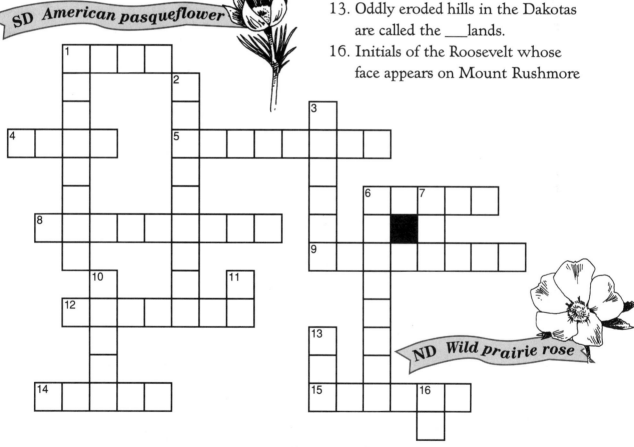

SD *American pasqueflower*

ND *Wild prairie rose*

Word List

AIM	Black	Garrison	Horse	TR
Bad	corn	gold	Missouri	wheat
Bismarck	Custer	Homestake	Rushmore	Wounded
	Dakota	Homestead	SD	

IOWA, KANSAS, AND NEBRASKA

The states of Iowa, Kansas, and Nebraska are grouped along the Missouri River at the center of the United States. In fact, Kansas contains the center of the U.S.'s forty-eight adjoining states. These three states are mostly flat farm country. Iowa has the richest soil and most wet climate. Nebraska and Kansas include part of the Great Plains and are a little higher and drier with harsher winters. Big thunderstorms are a feature of the weather in all these states, sometimes accompanied by tornadoes.

Iowa, which is farther east, was settled earlier than the other two states and was admitted to the Union in 1846, with Des Moines as its capital. Homesteading and the expansion of the railroad brought settlers to Kansas and Nebraska. Congress decided to let the people of Kansas decide whether to enter the nation as a free or slave state. The settlers fought real battles over the issue, and the state gained the nickname "Bleeding Kansas." At last, Kansas was admitted to the Union as a free state, with Topeka as its capital. Nebraska joined the United States after the Civil War. The nation's only unicameral (one-house) state legislature meets to make Nebraska's laws in its capital, Lincoln.

All three states are well known for their agriculture. Iowa grows more corn and raises more hogs than any other state. It is also the place where rolled oats became the first quick breakfast cereal. The biggest cereal-making plant in the world today is in Cedar Rapids, Iowa. Kansas rivals North Dakota for the nation's largest total wheat harvest. Huge cattle ranches cover much of the land in Nebraska and Kansas.

Life has been changing for families in farm states over the past few decades. Many Iowans, for example, now work at service jobs such as those in the insurance industry. Many people in Nebraska and Kansas work in manufacturing. In Wichita, Kansas's biggest city, for instance, workers put together more than half of the world's private airplanes.

Across

3. River that forms part of the border of Iowa, Nebraska, and Kansas
5. Main crop in Iowa
6. Largest city in Kansas
8. Term for a single-house legislature; they have one in Nebraska
10. State directly north of Kansas
11. Form of transportation that helped settle Nebraska and Kansas

12. Shape of most of the land in Iowa, Nebraska, and Kansas
14. Kind of transport built in Wichita
15. Iowa leads in raising these animals.

Down

1. Capital of Nebraska
2. Iowa, Kansas, and Nebraska are near the center of the North American

   _____ .
4. Many Iowans work in this service industry.
5. In _____ Rapids, Iowa, is the largest breakfast-cereal plant.
6. Main crop in Kansas
7. Nickname for Kansas Territory during slavery conflict
9. Form of oats; the first quick cereal
12. In this kind of state, more people are getting manufacturing or service jobs today.
13. Term for an area including Kansas: Tornado _____

Tornado Alley

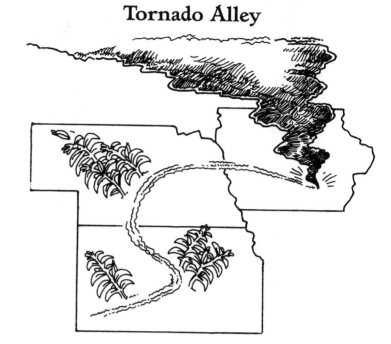

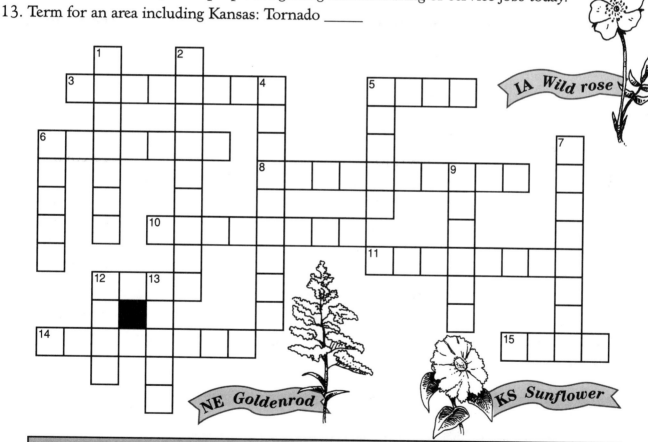

IA Wild rose

NE Goldenrod

KS Sunflower

Word List

airplane	Cedar	flat	Missouri	unicameral
Alley	continent	hogs	Nebraska	wheat
Bleeding	corn	insurance	railroad	Wichita
	farm	Lincoln	rolled	

MINNESOTA, WISCONSIN, AND MICHIGAN

Minnesota, Wisconsin, and Michigan are along the northern border of the United States, near the Great Lakes. The three states don't have many mountains, but all have some hills and plenty of streams and lakes. Minnesota claims more lakes than any other state: over 10,000!

Before the American Revolution, waterways served as highways to Native Americans, explorers, and fur traders in the Great Lakes region. Steamboats brought loads of immigrants, especially Scandinavians to Minnesota and Germans to Wisconsin. Today, the area's lakes and rivers are still major shipping routes.

Almost a hundred years ago, in Michigan, Henry Ford became the first American to make an affordable car using the assembly line. Soon Detroit became the car-manufacturing capital of the world. So many people poured into the state to work in auto-related industries that the population of Michigan ballooned, and it is now about twice that of Minnesota or Wisconsin. Even smaller cities like Flint and Lansing, the capital, took part in car making. Although cars and trucks are still built in Michigan, many autoworkers have had to look for other jobs because of increasing foreign competition.

In Wisconsin, dairy farms are everywhere and cheese is an important product. So is beer, first made in this state from traditional German recipes. Milwaukee, Wisconsin's largest city, can ship its products on Lake Michigan. The capital, Madison, lies inland.

The Mississippi River begins in central Minnesota. The state's biggest cities—Minneapolis and St. Paul, the capital—lie across from each other on the river. These "Twin Cities" bustle with business and the arts, and they are home to more than a dozen colleges. The Mall of America in Bloomington also attracts many visitors.

These three states also have a wild side. They offer fishing, hunting, boating, and hiking. Isle Royale, Michigan's national park in Lake Superior, once had one of the world's largest herds of moose.

Across

1. Milwaukee ships its products on this lake.
3. Michigan city where the Ford Motor Company began
7. Sport popular in north central states that you can do on water or ice
8. Mall of _____, the mammoth mall in Minnesota
10. Isle Royale is known for its herd of this animal.
13. The _____ line is a quick way of putting cars together.

28

14. There are over a dozen of these educational institutions in the Twin Cities.
15. Minnesota is the state with the most of these natural features.
16. Abbreviation of the first part of the name of Minnesota's capital

Down

1. Capital of Wisconsin
2. Ethnic group that settled much of Wisconsin
4. First word of the nickname for the cities Minneapolis and St. Paul
5. Michigan's population is about _____ as big as Wisconsin's or Minnesota's.
6. Capital of Michigan
7. Brand of the first Michigan-made affordable car
9. Country directly north from Minnesota and Michigan
11. Common Wisconsin dairy product
12. There are fewer of these in the U.S. auto industry today.

Word List

America	cheese	Ford	Lansing	St.
assembly	colleges	Germans	Madison	twice
Canada	Detroit	jobs	Michigan	Twin
	fishing	lakes	moose	

MISSOURI AND ARKANSAS

Missouri and Arkansas lie along the western side of the Mississippi River and share a range of low mountains and hills, or highlands, called the Ozarks. South of the Ozarks in Arkansas are the Ouachita Mountains. They are full of water springs, including 47 hot ones at beautiful Hot Springs National Park.

These two states were part of the Louisiana Purchase, the huge piece of land sold to the United States by France in 1803. The city of St. Louis, Missouri, became a midwestern hub and a gateway for settlement of the West. At the far western edge of Missouri is Kansas City. This former cow town, now larger in population than St. Louis, still has a western look. Missouri's capital, small Jefferson City, lies in the center of the state.

Both states also have a foot in the southern region. During the Civil War, citizens from both states fought on both sides of the conflict, although Arkansas left the Union and Missouri did not. Much later, in the 1950s, Arkansas was in the spotlight during the struggle for civil rights. The United States Supreme Court ruled that public schools must accept students without regard to their race. In many places across the South, including Arkansas, black and white students had been attending separate schools. After the court ruling, several black students braved angry crowds to enroll at Central High School in Little Rock, the state capital, for the first time.

In the past, farming was the main way of life in both states. It remains a chief industry in Missouri, where nearly every crop grows. Manufacturing is now the most important industry in Arkansas. People there make a living processing food, making electrical appliances, and making paper, among other things. The Wal-Mart chain of stores got its start in the state. Today, however, Arkansas may be most famous as the birthplace of Bill Clinton, a former governor who was elected president of the United States in 1992 and 1996.

Across

2. Initials of Missouri's westernmost big city
4. Missouri's capital: _____ City
6. He was an Arkansas governor before he became a U.S. president.
10. Economic activity now more important than farming in Arkansas
13. The Ozarks are ____lands in both states.
14. Major Arkansas product; used in schools
15. First word in the name of Arkansas's capital
16. Three-letter abbreviation for Arkansas
17. Arkansas has the only mine for these in the nation.

Down

The Gateway Arch in St. Louis, Missouri, reminds people of the city's history as a gateway for settlement of the West.

1. Missouri and Arkansas lie along this bank of the Mississippi River.
3. Name of the Little Rock high school spotlighted in the Civil Rights era
5. Still a major economic activity in Missouri
7. Both Arkansas and Missouri were part of the _____ Purchase.
8. Opposite of cold; what some Arkansas springs are
9. Mountains in southern Arkansas
11. Name of the monument arch in St. Louis
12. Popular dessert food introduced at the 1904 St. Louis World's Fair: _____-cream cone

Ice-cream cones were first served at the World's Fair in St. Louis, Missouri, in 1904.

AR Apple blossom

Arkansas has the nation's only diamond mine.

MO Hawthorn

Word List

Ark.	diamonds	hot	Little	paper
Central	farming	ice	Louisiana	west
Clinton	Gateway	Jefferson	manufacturing	
	high	KC	Ouachita	

ILLINOIS

Illinois is a busy state with farms, factories, and a successful transportation system. Illinois is the sixth most populous state.

Throughout Illinois's history, transportation routes have been the key to its success. The Mississippi River on the west and the Ohio River on the southeast border have allowed Illinois farmers and manufacturers to ship and sell goods from Canada to New Orleans and around the world. Even more valuable is the port of Chicago, one of the largest on the Great Lakes, with easy shipping routes eastward. The railroads gave Illinois a big economic boost as they brought grain and cattle from the West to Chicago for sale to eastern cities. Today, interstate truck routes and airplanes have joined the transportation web.

The city of Chicago, third largest in the nation after New York and Los Angeles, is a very exciting place. The first skyscraper was built there, and today, Chicago is home to the tallest building in the nation, the Sears Tower. Inside some of the skyscrapers, bankers are at work: This is the financial center of the Midwest. Once, poet Carl Sandburg called Chicago "hog butcher to the world." The slaughterhouses may have moved, but the Chicago Board of Trade remains the world's largest market for trading in grain and meat. O'Hare International Airport is among the busiest in the world. Culture in Chicago is lively, too. The city hums with jazz and the blues. The Art Institute of Chicago houses one of the finest art collections in the nation. And the Chicago Bulls basketball team is one of the nation's most popular.

There is a quieter side of Illinois south of Chicago. Most of the flat, fertile plains are farmland. Springfield, the state capital, sits in the middle of the state. There, you can visit memorials to Abraham Lincoln, perhaps the state's most famous citizen. To the south are hilly areas with woods and lakes.

Across

1. Capital of Illinois
4. Weather feature that gave Chicago its nickname
5. A famous art collection is at the Art _____ of Chicago.
8. Chicago's pro basketball team
10. The _____ Tower is the nation's tallest building.
11. Most Illinois farms are on this geographical feature.
13. River that helps form Illinois's southeast border
16. More recent form of transportation for Illinois products
17. Direction in which most goods are shipped from Chicago

Down

Chicago is called the Windy City for a good reason!

1. Last name of the poet who called Chicago "hog butcher to the world"
2. U.S. president memorialized in Springfield
3. Third largest city in the United States
6. Kind of tall building invented in Chicago
7. Along with jazz, a popular form of music in Chicago
9. Bumpy geographic features found in southern Illinois
12. Illinois's national rank in population
14. Name of one of the world's busiest airports; located in Chicago
15. The Chicago Board of _____ deals with large-scale grain and meat buying.

IL Native violet

Word List				
airplane	Chicago	Lincoln	Sandburg	Springfield
blues	east	O'Hare	Sears	Trade
Bulls	hills	Ohio	sixth	wind
	Institute	plains	skyscraper	

INDIANA AND OHIO

Soon after the Revolutionary War, Americans began to move across the Appalachian Mountains to the Ohio River valley and the land between it and the Great Lakes. This piece of land was soon made into states according to the Northwest Ordinance. This law, passed by Congress, allowed new states to enter the Union as equals of the original states if they met certain conditions. In 1803, Ohio was the first state created under these rules; land just to the west of Ohio became the state of Indiana.

Ohio grew in population more quickly than Indiana, and today, Ohio is full of cities both large and small. The largest cities in these two states were founded near water transportation. Cleveland became an industrial giant at the northern border of Ohio on Lake Erie, and Cincinnati grew as a major shipping point for goods on the Ohio River to the south. In Indiana, the city of Gary on Lake Michigan was closely linked with Chicago's trade.

Most land in Ohio and Indiana was scraped flat by glaciers thousands of years ago and is good for farming. In the east and south of Ohio, the Appalachian Plateau rises as a hilly region with steep ravines. Much of this land is covered with forests, and coal and oil are found there. Hills continue along the Ohio River at the southern borders of Ohio and Indiana. Huge salt deposits lie near Lake Erie, and beautiful limestone is quarried in Indiana. Service industries and manufacturing, such as steelmaking, are very important in both Indiana and Ohio.

Indianapolis, the capital and largest city of Indiana, is famous for its Indianapolis 500 auto race. Ohio State University, located in Columbus, the capital and largest city in Ohio, draws students and football fans to its large campus. The city of Cleveland, Ohio, has built a new theater district to draw visitors downtown.

Across

1. The Appalachian Plateau rises in the south and ____ of Ohio.
4. Capital of Indiana
5. Initials for the large university in Columbus
10. Capital of Ohio
11. Lake that forms the northern border of Ohio
13. Cleveland has created a new downtown district for this form of entertainment.
15. Large city on the Ohio River in the state of Ohio
17. The Northwest _____ set rules for territories becoming states.
18. Deposits of this mineral lie near Lake Erie.

Down

2. Mountain chain separating eastern states from Ohio
3. Indiana city near Chicago on Lake Michigan
6. Ohio became a _____ in 1803.
7. Beautiful building stone quarried in Indiana
8. Opposite of northern; the hilly border of both Ohio and Indiana
9. These scraped land flat in Ohio and Indiana.
12. The Indianapolis 500 is a famous car ___.
14. An important part of the economy in both Indiana and Ohio
16. A hard fuel mineral found in the Appalachian Plateau

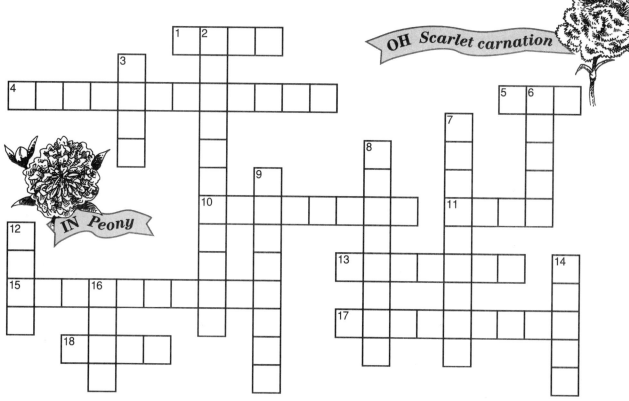

OH *Scarlet carnation*

IN *Peony*

Word List

Appalachian	Columbus	glaciers	OSU	state
Cincinnati	east	Indianapolis	race	steel
coal	Erie	limestone	salt	theater
	Gary	Ordinance	southern	

TENNESSEE, KENTUCKY, AND WEST VIRGINIA

The Appalachian Mountains extend all the way from Maine to Georgia. They take up much of the land of Tennessee, Kentucky, and West Virginia. In fact, West Virginia is the most mountainous state east of the Rockies. You can enjoy the beauty of these mountains in Great Smoky Mountains National Park in Tennessee and North Carolina.

Settlement of these areas began when the earliest pioneers, including Daniel Boone, crossed the mountains from the East. Kentucky and Tennessee became states in the 1790s. West Virginia was then part of the state of Virginia. It did not become a state until the Civil War, when people in this region decided not to secede from, or leave, the Union with the rest of Virginia.

The beautiful Appalachians have yielded plentiful coal and wood products, but they are hard to farm, and miners in the mountains have faced bad conditions and long periods without work. Still, the mountain people have a proud cultural heritage including folk music, crafts, and stories.

Manufacturing has become the main source of income in all three states. Tourists also enjoy the mountains and come through historic towns like the capitals— Charleston, West Viginia; Frankfort, Kentucky; or Nashville, Tennessee. Some traditional ways of making a living are still thriving. In Kentucky, Thoroughbred horses are still raised and sold around the world from the Bluegrass region, and bourbon whiskey continues to be made. Tennessee has benefited from the dam and lake system created by the national Tennessee Valley Authority to create inexpensive electricity, a project begun in the 1930s. Yet cotton still grows as it did a hundred years ago in eastern Tennessee. The first trade highways for these states were the Ohio and Mississippi Rivers, which continue to carry goods today.

Across

1. Crop traditionally grown in eastern Tennessee
3. Initials of the most mountainous state east of the Rockies
4. Kind of racehorse raised in Kentucky
7. First name of an early Kentucky pioneer
8. Nashville is called the capital of country _____.
10. Economic activity that brings most money to Kentucky, West Virginia, and Tennessee
13. Capital of Kentucky
14. The Great _____ Mountains National Park lies partly in Tennessee.
15. Capital of Tennessee

Down

Nashville, Tennessee, is the capital of country music.

1. Capital of West Virginia
2. Initials of the state that shares a national park with Tennessee
3. The forested mountains have yielded many products made of this.
4. Initials of the government system of dams and lakes along the Tennessee River
5. Kind of grass; name of Kentucky's horse country
6. Sightseer; there are many in these three states

9. Artificial ones have been created by dams in Tennessee.
11. West Virginia became a state after it refused to leave the _____ in the Civil War.
12. Mineral most mined in the Appalachian Mountains

The Appalachians, a popular area with tourists, are known for coal mining.

TN Iris

WV Rhododendron

KY Goldenrod

Word List

Bluegrass	cotton	manufacturing	Smoky	Union
Charleston	Daniel	music	Thoroughbred	wood
coal	Frankfort	Nashville	tourist	WV
	lakes	NC	TVA	

MISSISSIPPI AND LOUISIANA

Mississippi and Louisiana sit on either side of the Mississippi River as it flows to its end in the Gulf of Mexico. In these states, you can relive the history of the Deep South—and see how the South has changed.

Mississippi's first very profitable crop was cotton, and cotton remains "king" of agriculture in the state today. That is because the state is perfectly suited to big cotton farms: The land is flat and fertile, the temperature warm all year, and rainfall plentiful. Today, however, most Mississippians work in services or manufacturing rather than in agriculture. A small number of workers and machinery now do the farmwork once done by slaves under the old plantation system. Near Natchez, you can see historic mansions built by plantation owners before the Civil War. And at Vicksburg, a port on the Mississippi, you can visit the site of the Civil War battle that marked a turning point in the war in favor of the Union.

Mississippi includes the forested Piney Woods region, where trees are cut down to make paper, turpentine, and other products. Along the Gulf Coast, shrimping and fishing boats are at work. The capital, Jackson, lies in the middle of the state and is the largest city.

Louisiana is famous throughout the world, mostly because of the colorful city of New Orleans. Louisiana's heritage is largely French: It was the cultural center of the Louisiana Purchase. The economic strength of the state was first based on its control of trade at the mouth of the Mississippi. River barges and oceangoing vessels still churn the river waters between Baton Rouge, the capital, and New Orleans. Trade continues to be the most important business in the state, followed closely by tourism. People flock to New Orleans to hear good jazz in the city where it was born, and to enjoy delicious foods, such as the soup called gumbo, that combine French and American flavors. Many tourists also come to the city each year for Mardi Gras, New Orleans's biggest holiday, which is celebrated with parades and fun costumes.

Across

2. Slave labor was used to support this kind of large farm.
7. Second word in the name of New Orleans's famous holiday
9. Mississippi's top economic activity today, along with manufacturing
11. Nickname for cotton in the South
12. A forested area of Mississippi is called the _____ Woods region.
14. What parading people wear at Mardi Gras
15. French and American soup served in New Orleans
16. Near this city, you can see mansions from before the Civil War.
17. Body of water into which the Mississippi flows: _____ of Mexico

Down

Scenes from Mississippi and Louisiana

1. Capital of Mississippi
3. A liquid product gained from Mississippi trees
4. Initials of the city at the mouth of the Mississippi
5. Mississippi gets plenty of this to water its crops.
6. Louisiana's main economic activity, in the past and today
8. Location of a major Civil War battle in Mississippi
9. Edible sea animal harvested from the Gulf of Mexico, along with fish
10. First word in the name of Louisiana's capital
13. Nation that put its cultural stamp on New Orleans

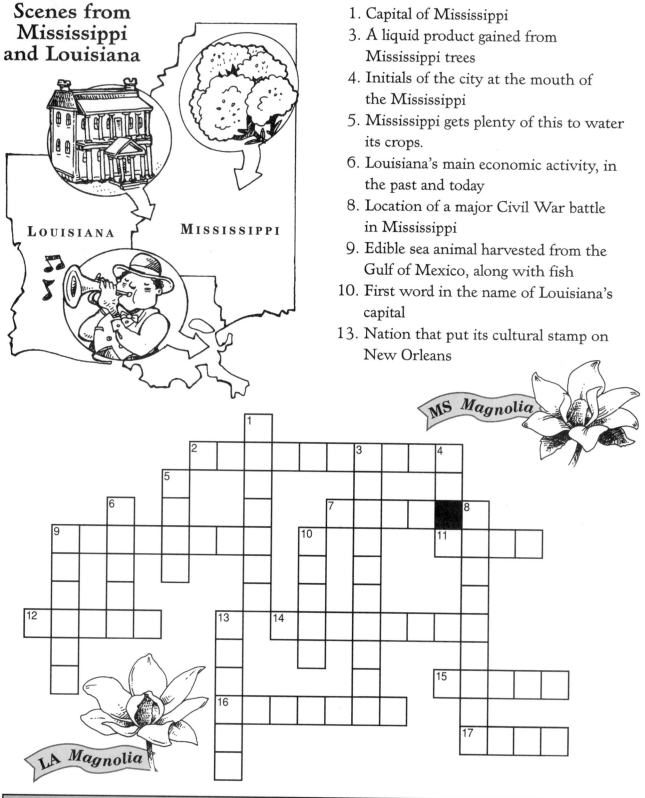

LOUISIANA

MISSISSIPPI

MS Magnolia

LA Magnolia

Word List

Baton	Gras	king	plantation	trade
costumes	Gulf	Natchez	rain	turpentine
France	gumbo	NO	services	Vicksburg
	Jackson	Piney	shrimp	

ALABAMA AND GEORGIA

Alabama and Georgia are neighbors in the heart of the American South. Coastal plains cover the southern two-thirds of both states, although the land rises in a rolling area called the Piedmont. North of the Piedmont are hills and mountains that are part of the Appalachians. Settlers quickly found that the Piedmont and plains were prime cotton-growing lands. Georgia, one of the original thirteen colonies, developed an economy based on the plantation system and slave labor. This way of life extended to the area that became Alabama. Both states were part of the Confederacy during the Civil War. There have been many changes in both states since that time.

Boll weevils, insects that eat cotton crops, destroyed cotton harvests during the 1920s. Today, there is even a monument to the boll weevil in Alabama! Farmers tried other crops, such as peanuts, and some former farmland was returned to forest. Forest products such as paper and building lumber are important to both states today. Manufacturing and services now employ most people. Birmingham, Alabama, is a major iron and steel producer, partly because the coal, iron ore, and limestone needed to make steel are located in the surrounding area. Birmingham is now the largest city in the state.

In 1955, a bus boycott in Montgomery, Alabama's capital, touched off the Civil Rights movement. In time, that movement led to voting rights and to more opportunities in jobs and education for African Americans throughout the United States.

Atlanta, the capital of Georgia, has become the urban center of the southeastern part of the United States. Atlanta has always been important as a transportation hub and serves as the headquarters of Delta Air Lines. Today, almost half of all Georgians live within the greater metropolitan area of Atlanta.

Both Alabama and Georgia have areas of coast. Alabama's is on the Gulf of Mexico, where fishing boats come in to Mobile Bay. Georgia's Atlantic coast attracts tourists, as does the wildlife refuge in the Okefenokee Swamp.

Across

2. One crop that replaced cotton after the boll weevils attacked
3. The Civil Rights movement gained strength in the Montgomery ___ boycott.
6. The Civil Rights movement resulted in African Americans having better _____ in government.
10. Name of a swamp that is a wildlife refuge in southern Georgia
11. Abbreviation that follows civil rights activitist Martin Luther King's name
13. About this fraction of Georgians live in the greater metropolitan area of Atlanta.
14. Atlanta serves as an urban center for this national region.

15. Before it was a state, Georgia was this.
16. Name of national airline headquartered in Atlanta

Down

Civil rights leader Martin Luther King, Jr., speaking to the press on March 19, 1956, about the bus boycott in Montgomery, Alabama

1. Capital of Georgia
2. Rolling area north of the coastal plains in Alabama and Georgia
3. Largest city in Alabama
4. Iron ___ , located near Birmingham, is used in making steel.
5. Capital of Alabama
7. Some former plantation land is now part of this natural resource.
8. Name of Alabama's bay on the Gulf of Mexico
9. Second word in the name of the insect for which Alabama has a monument
12. Part of the cotton plant and first name of the insect that destroyed crops in the 1920s

GA Cherokee rose

AL Camellia

Word List

Atlanta	bus	half	Okefenokee	representation
Birmingham	colony	Jr.	ore	Southeast
boll	Delta	Mobile	peanuts	weevil
	forest	Montgomery	Piedmont	

FLORIDA

What is the most popular single-attraction tourist destination in the world? You can probably guess the answer: Disney World in Florida. Florida also has so many other attractions that it's no wonder tourism is the state's top moneymaker.

Part of Florida's appeal is in its climate and location. The state is a large peninsula that extends southward into the Atlantic Ocean. Attached to the peninsula is a northwestern panhandle of Gulf Coast land where Tallahassee, the state capital, lies. Because of its shape, Florida has an enormous continuous coastline that attracts people to its beaches and boat docks. Florida's climate is warm all year. In the far southern part of the state, including many small islands called the Florida Keys, the climate is tropical, which means it changes little with the seasons. Even in northern Florida, winter temperatures rarely fall below freezing. However, Florida is often in the path of hurricanes.

Florida caught the eye of Europeans in the early 1500s. Spain established the first permanent settlement in North America at St. Augustine, on the northeast coast. The Spanish first grew oranges in Florida; today, citrus fruits are the state's most valuable crop. Beginning in the 1800s, Florida became a destination for "snowbirds," people escaping from winter in the northeastern states. Others come to Florida to retire. Large communities of retired people have increased the population of cities like St. Petersburg. Florida has also become home to Hispanic people from south of the U.S. border, including many Cubans.

Visitors to Florida are likely to stop in the Orlando area, where there are many theme parks, including Universal Studios and Sea World. East of Orlando on the coast is the Kennedy Space Center at Cape Canaveral.

Across

1. Country that established the first permanent settlement in North America
6. Capital of Florida
8. Florida city where many theme parks are located
9. Name of islands below the southern tip of the Florida peninsula
10. Many people go to Florida to live when they _____ from their jobs.
13. People who winter in Florida's warm climate are given this nickname.
14. Severe kind of storm that sometimes blasts Florida
15. Temperatures all over Florida are this.
16. The northwestern Gulf Coast strip of Florida is shaped like a ___handle.

Down

1. Universal _____ is a theme park in Florida.
2. Kind of water and land animal you might see in the Everglades
3. Name of the "World" that is the world's top tourist destination; in Florida
4. Name of the Florida cape where spacecraft are launched into space
5. Florida city with many retired people: St. _____
7. Chief economic activity in Florida
11. Many immigrants from this Caribbean island have come to live in Florida.
12. Orlando theme park featuring ocean creatures: ___ World
13. Kind of land within Everglades National Park

At Everglades National Park, you can take an airboat through swampland to see pelicans, alligators, and other creatures.

FL Orange blossom

Word List

alligator	Disney	pan	snowbirds	Tallahassee
Canaveral	hurricane	Petersburg	Spain	tourism
Cuba	Keys	retire	Studios	warm
	Orlando	Sea	swamp	

NORTH CAROLINA AND SOUTH CAROLINA

Both the Carolinas have miles and miles of beaches. In both states, the wide coastal plain ends at the slightly higher, rolling red-clay country called the Piedmont. The Piedmont is divided from the plain along the "fall line," where early mill owners once set their waterwheels to take advantage of the descending streams. Many towns—such as both state capitals, Raleigh, North Carolina, and Columbia, South Carolina—grew up naturally along this fall line. West of the Piedmont lies the Appalachian mountain chain. North Carolina holds the chain's highest peaks, including the tallest, Mount Mitchell.

The Carolinas were among the thirteen original colonies. In fact, the first English settlement in the Americas was founded on Roanoke Island off North Carolina in 1585—although it mysteriously disappeared soon after. By the early 1800s, cotton and tobacco plantations supported by slaves had become a way of life. The first shots of the Civil War were fired at Fort Sumter, South Carolina, and after the war, a long period of poverty followed. In the years following the war, many textile mills employed people, as they do today, although low wages and competition from abroad have been problems.

Today, most Carolina people work in tourism and manufacturing. Tobacco is the biggest crop, and cigarette making is a large industry, especially around Raleigh in North Carolina. Since the 1970s, the population of each state has been growing, partly because of new electronics industries and university growth. In North Carolina, a "research triangle" has grown up around the University of North Carolina at Chapel Hill, Duke University, and North Carolina State. And visitors come to the Carolinas not only for the beaches but also to see historic sites such as the colonial era gardens and homes in Charleston, South Carolina.

Across

5. South Carolina city famous for its colonial era gardens and houses
6. Low _____ have been a problem for workers in Carolina textile mills.
8. The first mills along the fall line depended on this kind of power.
9. Private university that forms part of the North Carolina research triangle
10. The islands off North Carolina are called the _____ Banks.
13. Capital of North Carolina
14. Major crop in both Carolinas
15. Starting place of the Civil War in South Carolina: _____ Sumter
16. Area formed by three universities in North Carolina, famous for research

Down

1. These coastal features attract tourists to the Carolinas.
2. Name of the line between the coastal plain and the Piedmont
3. Name of the tallest Appalachian mountain
4. These tobacco products are made around Raleigh.
5. Capital of South Carolina
7. Salty ones help separate the Outer Banks from the North Carolina mainland.
11. North Carolina was the site of the _____ English settlement in America.
12. Means the same as "increase"; what happened to the Carolina population after 1970
17. Initials of the Carolina with the highest mountains

North Carolina's Outer Banks

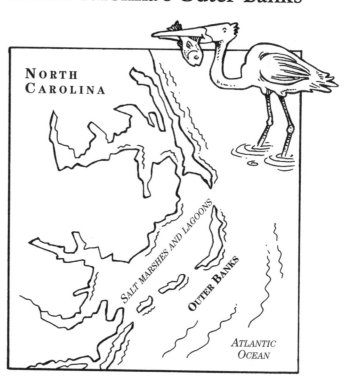

NORTH CAROLINA

SALT MARSHES AND LAGOONS

OUTER BANKS

ATLANTIC OCEAN

SC *Yellow jessamine*

NC *Flowering dogwood*

Word List				
beaches	Columbia	Fort	NC	triangle
Charleston	Duke	growth	Outer	wages
cigarettes	fall	marshes	Raleigh	water
	first	Mitchell	tobacco	

45

VIRGINIA AND MARYLAND

Virginia and Maryland have a geography similar to the rest of the states that line the Atlantic Ocean in the South. Flat coastal plains, sometimes called the tidewater region, give way to the slightly higher, rolling Piedmont. On the western edge of each state is part of the Appalachian range named the Blue Ridge. In Virginia, it is called the ridge and valley region. Maryland has a special physical feature, the Chesapeake Bay. The part of Maryland east of the bay is known as the Eastern Shore. Only the southeastern tip of Maryland extends out to the Atlantic, where Ocean City welcomes beachgoers. Between Virginia and Maryland flows the Potomac, on which Washington, D.C., is located. The national capital strongly affects both states.

The capital of Maryland, Annapolis, is a small city on the western shore of the Chesapeake. Baltimore, to the north on the same side, is by far Maryland's biggest city. The area between Baltimore and Washington, D.C., is so urbanized that it is really one huge metropolitan area. In the past, Baltimore was host to heavy industries, but today, many people work for government agencies or in computer software or biotech industries.

Virginia is a much larger state, but it, too, is home to many government institutions and businesses that serve the national government. You can still visit many places to remember Virginia's rich history, such as Jamestown, site of the first lasting English colony, and colonial Williamsburg. The capital of the state, Richmond, was once the capital of the Confederacy. Civil War battlefields all over the state show how hard the war was fought there.

A good place to see natural Virginia is in Shenandoah National Park, where hardwood forests blanket the Blue Ridge. They turn lovely colors in the fall.

Across

5. Capital of Virginia
8. Largest city in Maryland
9. Name of a national park in Virginia
11. Shellfish that walks sideways and lives in Chesapeake Bay
12. The part of Maryland on the east side of Chesapeake Bay is called the Eastern _____.
13. A good season in which to visit the Blue Ridge in Virginia
14. Site of a Civil War fight; there are many in Virginia
16. First word in the name of a Maryland city on the Atlantic coast
17. The west part of Virginia is called the _____ and valley region.

MARYLAND

CHESAPEAKE BAY

ATLANTIC OCEAN

VIRGINIA

Fishermen work the waters of Chesapeake Bay, gathering crabs, clams, oysters, and many kinds of fish, but water pollution is endangering the catch.

Down

1. Virginia colonial town open to visitors
2. River that forms the border between Maryland and Virginia
3. Name of the first lasting English settlement, located in Virginia
4. Name of the large bay in the middle of Maryland
6. Color found in the name given to mountains in western Virginia and Maryland
7. Capital of Maryland
10. Initials of the district between Virginia and Maryland
11. Richmond, Virginia, was once this in the Confederacy.
15. Name given to the coastal plain: ____water

MD Black-eyed Susan

VA Dogwood

Word List

Annapolis	blue	DC	Potomac	Shore
Baltimore	capital	fall	Richmond	tide
battlefield	Chesapeake	Jamestown	ridge	Williamsburg
	crab	Ocean	Shenandoah	

PENNSYLVANIA

The English Quaker William Penn founded the colony of Pennsylvania, which means "Penn's Woods." He invited people from many parts of Europe to come and farm peacefully together, and he tried to treat the Native Americans fairly. Today, Pennsylvania is the nation's fifth largest state in population. Even though the state has so many people, plenty of countryside remains for hiking, skiing, and hunting in state parks and reserves. In the middle of Pennsylvania, the small city of Harrisburg serves as the state's capital.

The state includes a flat coastal plains area, a higher lowland called the Piedmont, then the Appalachian Mountains, also called the Alleghenies in this state. On the western side of the state, the Appalachian Plateau, a hilly region, descends to the Great Lakes area and across the border with Ohio. The richest land is in the southeast, "Pennsylvania Dutch" country. The Dutch are really "Deutsch," or Germans, whose ancestors responded to advertisements made in Europe by Penn. Pennsylvania is a leader in dairy products, chickens, eggs, apples, mushrooms—and Christmas trees!

The state has two major cities, Philadelphia in the east and Pittsburgh in the west. Philadelphia, the largest, was actually planned by William Penn. It is still a port and a commercial center, as he meant it to be, but now it is one of the world's great cities. Many of the nation's largest corporations have headquarters in the city. Some of the great events in U.S. history took place here, including the writing of the Declaration of Independence and the Constitution. Today, you can visit the sites of these events and others within Independence National Historic Park.

Pittsburgh grew up where the Allegheny and Monongahela Rivers meet to form the Ohio River. The city sits atop underground coalfields that, along with iron ore, built the city as a steelmaker. Today, some steel is still made in the area, but the city's economy is now based on services, technology, and education (colleges and universities).

Across

2. Pennsylvania's largest city
5. Pennsylvania leads in growing these for Christmas.
6. Term for large businesses; many have headquarters in Philadelphia
8. Name of the national historic park where you can see famous Philadelphia buildings
10. Summer activity you can do in Pennsylvania parks
14. The founder of Pennsylvania was one.
15. Pittsburgh grew up as a maker of this.
16. Pennsylvania's chief western city
17. Term for milk and milk products; Pennsylvania produces a lot

Down

1. River that joins the Monongahela to form the Ohio River
3. Capital of Pennsylvania
4. *Pennsylvania* means "Penn's _____."
6. Pittsburgh is located right on top of this underground material.
7. Pennsylvania's number among the states in population size
9. Educational institutions that contribute to the economy of Pittsburgh
11. Leading Pennsylvania farm product made by chickens
12. The "Pennsylvania Dutch" are really of this ethnic background.
13. Founder of the colony of Pennsylvania

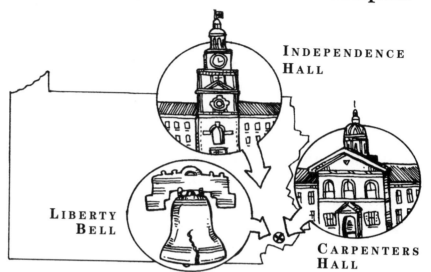

Important Historic Sites in Philadelphia

INDEPENDENCE HALL

LIBERTY BELL

CARPENTERS HALL

PA Mountain laurel

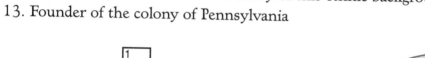

Word List

Allegheny	corporations	German	Penn	steel
coal	dairy	Harrisburg	Philadelphia	trees
colleges	eggs	hike	Pittsburgh	Woods
	five	Independence	Quaker	

DELAWARE AND NEW JERSEY

W hat did Dela ware?" asks the old song. "She wore a New Jersey." In fact, these neighboring states have a lot in common. They share Delaware Bay and part of the Delaware River, which form the boundary between them. Both are old industrial states, with chemicals as a top product. Yet both states now depend less on industry, and more of the population is moving to suburban areas and to jobs in services. Both states have plenty of people: New Jersey is the most densely populated of all the states.

Delaware is the smallest of all the states except for Rhode Island. In 1787, Delaware was the first to ratify the U.S. Constitution, and so became the first state, with Dover as its capital. Much of southern Delaware remains quiet farm country, where chickens are the main product. Rehoboth, a town on the Atlantic, is a good place to enjoy the waves. Northern Delaware is much busier. Wilmington, at the mouth of the Delaware River, is the state's chief city. State laws give tax advantages to corporations, so many have located their headquarters there. Du Pont has headed the list of chemical companies in Delaware for a very long time. Today, it is Delaware's largest employer.

New Jersey lies between the giant cities of Philadelphia and New York, and much of its industry grew up along that line. Trenton, the capital, sits midway along this line on the Delaware River. New Jersey farms supply many of the needs of the people of New York City and of the nation. Most farmland is in the southern part of the state. Atlantic City, on the coast, has become famous for casino gambling. Hills and mountains in New Jersey's northwest section offer good places to ski and hike.

Across

1. Name of a prominent chemical company in Delaware
4. Delaware's largest city
6. What population is in New Jersey; opposite of sparse
7. Much of southern New Jersey is rural _____ country.
10. Capital of Delaware
11. Delaware city by the sea
13. Delaware laws give this kind of advantage to corporations.
14. Farm animals raised most in Delaware
15. First word in the name of the New Jersey city that has casino gambling

Major Water Routes

Down

1. Name of the bay and river that separate New Jersey and Delaware
2. Most New Jersey industries are located in a belt between New York City and _____.
3. Capital of New Jersey
5. Recreation such as skiing can be had in this part of New Jersey.
8. The _____ industry is important in both Delaware and New Jersey.
9. A barge going from New Jersey to New York would have to cross this river.
11. Initials of the only state smaller than Delaware
12. A ship taking the shortest route from Wilmington to Baltimore would pass through this.
16. Initials of the state where many New Jersey fruits and vegetables are sold

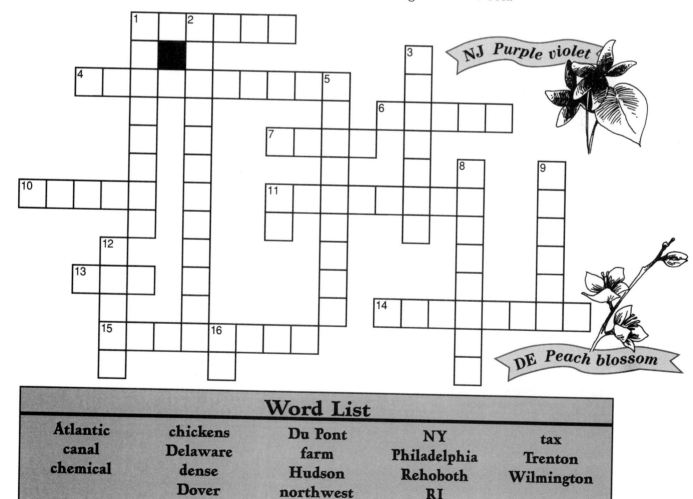

Word List

Atlantic	chickens	Du Pont	NY	tax
canal	Delaware	farm	Philadelphia	Trenton
chemical	dense	Hudson	Rehoboth	Wilmington
	Dover	northwest	RI	

NEW YORK

They call it the Big Apple. It's New York City, the biggest city in the United States and the cornerstone of a big, busy state. After the Revolutionary War, New York City served as the first capital of the new nation. The large harbor at New York City invited trade from the beginning, and it became even more important after the Erie Canal was opened in the 1820s. The canal ran eastward from Buffalo on the shore of Lake Erie to Albany, the state capital, located on the Hudson River. The canal, then the railroad, and then trucks took increasing loads of goods from the middle of the country via Great Lakes ports to New York City. There, goods were bought, sold, and shipped all over the country and the world. A chain of industrial cities grew up along this water and railroad route, including Buffalo, Rochester, Syracuse, Utica, and others.

Today, although heavy industries like steel have closed many of their plants, New York remains a leading state in manufacturing, wholesale trade, communication, and finance. Some leading products are books and magazines: New York is the nation's chief publishing city. Another leader is clothing. And at the Stock Exchange on Wall Street in New York City, you can see every kind of American business being traded, and feel the pulse of the American economy as a whole.

Tourism is also a big business in New York. People come to the Big Apple for theater, famous art museums, music, shopping, and fun. They also come to see historical sites such as the Statue of Liberty in New York Harbor and Ellis Island, where many immigrants first arrived in the United States. The state of New York also includes farmland and beautiful natural spots away from the cities. There are several thousand lakes in New York, including Lake Ontario, which is one of the largest.

Across

1. From the beginning, this haven for ships helped New York City trade.
3. Product of heavy industry; made less than in the past in New York
6. One of New York's largest lakes, along with Lake Erie
7. Name of forested mountains in the northeastern part of New York
8. Type of exchange on Wall Street
11. Visitors come to see this in museums in New York City.
12. Kind of land that produces crops; plenty remains in New York State
14. Name of the canal between Buffalo and Albany
16. Major city at the western end of the canal

Down

2. Form of transportation built alongside the Erie Canal route
3. Industrial city that developed because of the Erie Canal
4. The Statue of _____ stands in New York Harbor.
5. You read these; many are made in New York
7. Nickname for New York City: the Big _____
9. New York is a leading maker of this wearable product.
10. Bodies of water in central New York: the Finger _____
13. Capital of New York
15. Name of the island where many immigrants first landed

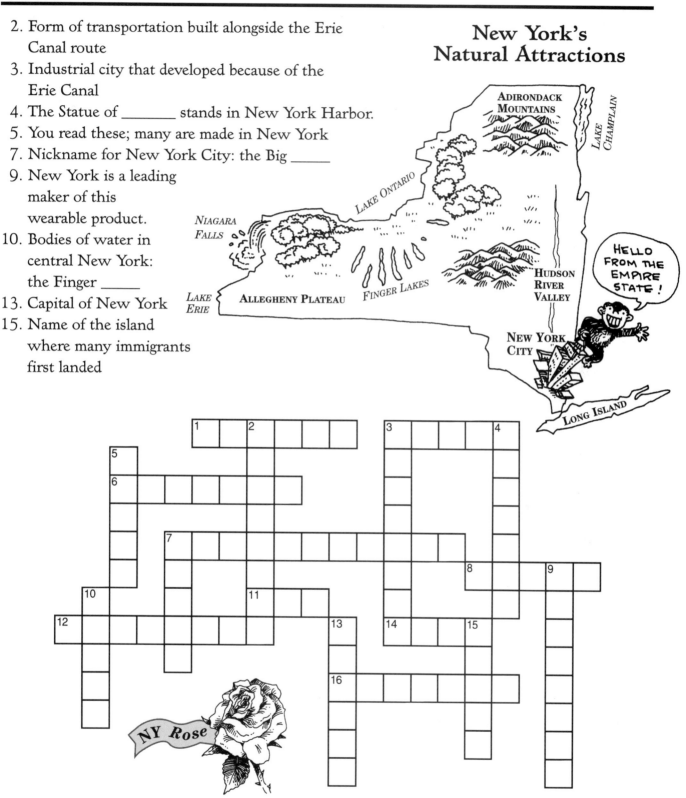

New York's Natural Attractions

ADIRONDACK MOUNTAINS

LAKE CHAMPLAIN

LAKE ONTARIO

NIAGARA FALLS

LAKE ERIE

ALLEGHENY PLATEAU

FINGER LAKES

HUDSON RIVER VALLEY

HELLO FROM THE EMPIRE STATE!

NEW YORK CITY

LONG ISLAND

NY Rose

Word List

Adirondacks	art	Ellis	Lakes	steel
Albany	books	Erie	Liberty	stock
Apple	Buffalo	farmland	Ontario	Syracuse
	clothing	harbor	railroad	

CONNECTICUT AND RHODE ISLAND

Both Connecticut and Rhode Island have rich colonial histories. Connecticut's first constitution, the Fundamental Orders, set rules under which the colony governed itself. The orders served as one model for the U.S. Constitution. Rhode Island, the nation's smallest state, was founded by people seeking religious freedom from the Puritans in Massachusetts. Rhode Island became the first colony to formally declare independence from Britain.

Both states have prospered because of their Atlantic coastlines. Connecticut's long, sheltered coast along Long Island Sound afforded good harbors such as New London and Mystic, famous for shipbuilding and whaling in the early 1800s. Today, many commuters to New York live in southern Connecticut, in towns like Stamford.

Rhode Island's harbors are mostly in huge Narragansett Bay. Newport, on an island in the bay, has long been famous as a resort town and has boat races and music festivals. Today, you can visit Newport mansions where the rich vacationed beginning in the mid-1700s. The port city of Providence, on the mainland, is the state capital. Many people there work at making costume jewelry. Long ago, Samuel Slater built the nation's first fabric mill in Rhode Island, and soon all New England was humming with such mills. Today, though, most Rhode Islanders work in service jobs.

Industry remains important in Connecticut, which is a large producer of aircraft engines, submarines, and helicopters. The fertile Connecticut River valley cuts a farming belt north to south through the middle of the state. Hartford, the capital, sits on the river. The headquarters for many insurance firms are located there. Much of the rest of the state is hilly, especially in the northwest. That part of the Appalachian highlands is called the Berkshires, known as a good place to see autumn leaves.

Across

2. Capital of Connecticut
4. Kind of jewelry made in Providence
7. Waterway off Connecticut's south shore: the Long Island _____
9. Connecticut's early constitution: the _____ Orders
11. Large sea animal once hunted from Connecticut ports
14. Name of Rhode Island's very large bay
15. Connecticut leads in producing this kind of engine.
16. Newport is located on one of these.
17. Famous university in New Haven, Connecticut

Down

1. Capital of Rhode Island
3. Popular boat event in Newport
5. Fancy house; you can visit old ones in Newport
6. Mountains in Connecticut's northwest

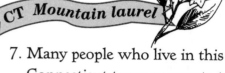

Famous Universities in Connecticut and Rhode Island

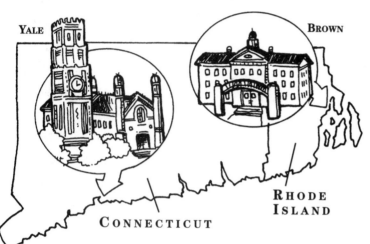

7. Many people who live in this Connecticut town commute to New York for work.
8. Many large companies in this business are headquartered in Hartford.
10. Last name of the man who built the first fabric mill in New England
12. The Berkshires are a good place to see colorful ones in autumn.
13. Well-known university in Providence, Rhode Island

RI *Violet*

Word List

aircraft	costume	island	Providence	Stamford
Berkshires	Fundamental	leaves	race	whale
Brown	Hartford	mansion	Slater	Yale
	insurance	Narragansett	Sound	

MASSACHUSETTS

Massachusetts has a history full of firsts. It was the first of the colonies to enjoy democracy and town meetings, the first to sponsor public schools, the first to have a college and a library, and the first to act against the British in the Revolutionary War. Many reminders of the state's rich history are available to the public today, including Old Sturbridge Village, a re-creation of a typical New England town in the 1830s.

Massachusetts remains an important state despite its small size. Boston, the capital of Massachusetts, is an important city for the New England region and the rest of the nation. Massachusetts is home to many of the nation's finest colleges, including Harvard University, the first university to be founded in the United States. High-tech computer and electronics businesses have settled near such research institutions as the Massachusetts Institute of Technology (MIT).

The land in Massachusetts is low in the east and rises toward the west. From the southeast corner of the state, the sandy Cape Cod peninsula stretches out in a hook shape. South of it are the large islands of Martha's Vineyard and Nantucket. While the peninsula and islands were once home to fishing and whaling industries, today they are summer vacation spots. Provincetown, a town at the tip of the Cape, is known for its arts and theater.

The flat eastern part of the state is thickly populated, but the soil is sandy and rocky. It's no wonder many New Englanders turned to fishing or manufacturing instead of farming. Today, services and trade provide most jobs, though there is still some fishing, chiefly for cod and lobster. Farms tend to raise specialty crops, such as cranberries. The most fertile part of the state is the Connecticut River valley, which runs north to south. On the western side of the Connecticut River, the land rises to the rolling hills of the Berkshires.

Across

2. Kind of free schools first established in Massachusetts
4. Where the Pilgrims landed; now site of a seventeenth-century living history "Plantation"
6. At Old _____ Village in Massachusetts, you can see how people lived during the 1830s.
9. Opposite of high; describes land in eastern Massachusetts
11. Specialty crop grown in Massachusetts, often used at Thanksgiving
12. Initials of an important research institute in Massachusetts
14. The Connecticut River _____ is a fertile area.
15. Massachusetts settlers were the first to have this kind of meeting.
16. Large island off the Massachusetts coast

Down

1. In Massachusetts, the Berkshires are mainly rolling _____.
2. Town on the tip of Cape Cod, famous for its theater

3. First word in the name of the hook-shaped Massachusetts peninsula
5. Massachusetts fishermen still gather this large shellfish.
7. Capital of Massachusetts
8. First college established in the United States
10. Boston is the chief city in the region of ___ England.
13. Eastern Massachusetts soil is sandy and _____.
15. Many Massachusetts businesses now are high _____.

Visitors can relive history at Plimoth Plantation, a re-creation of a 1627 Pilgrim village in Plymouth, Massachusetts.

MA Mayflower

Word List

Boston	Harvard	MIT	Provincetown	tech
Cape	hills	Nantucket	public	town
cranberries	lobster	New	rocky	valley
	low	Plymouth	Sturbridge	

NEW HAMPSHIRE, VERMONT, AND MAINE

New Hampshire, Vermont, and Maine make up the northeastern corner of the United States. They are all well known for their beautiful forests and mountains, and for their long, snowy winters attractive to skiers. Tourism is a major business in all three states. Though the states all have similar terrain, each has its own character.

New Hampshire was one of the original thirteen states. Its capital, Concord, is especially busy every four years because the state hosts the earliest presidential primary election in the nation. New Hampshire is also well known for its unusual tax laws: It has no state income tax or state sales tax. That is because most citizens of the state are conservative: They want to limit the powers of government.

Vermont was an area in dispute between New York and New Hampshire before Vermonters decided to form their own independent republic in 1777. Vermont helped fight the British in the American Revolution and afterward joined the Union as the fourteenth state. Vermont has no seacoast, though its largest city, Burlington, is on Lake Champlain. Montpelier, the capital, is in the center of the state. Vermont shares deposits of granite and marble with New Hampshire. Politically, however, the state is liberal: Most Vermonters want government to help solve problems.

The area that is known as Maine once belonged to Massachusetts, but it became a state on its own in 1820. Lumber industries are the major source of income. Portland is the largest city in Maine. In fact, most people live in the southwestern part of the state. L.L. Bean, the clothing and outdoor outfitter whose catalogs reach the whole country, is located in Freeport. North of the capital, Augusta, the population thins. Potato farms fill some northern counties. There are fewer fishermen along the coast than in the past, but the beauty of the area still draws many visitors.

Across

3. Capital of Vermont
6. Vermont city on Lake Champlain
8. High landform in Vermont, New Hampshire, and Maine
12. New Hampshire's early presidential primary is one.
13. New Hampshire has neither the sales nor the income kind of this.
14. Last word in name of one of the most famous businesses in Maine
15. This kind of resort makes money during winter in the mountains.
17. Name of the national park on Maine's northern coast
18. Cutting and processing this brings Maine people the most income.

Down

1. Before Vermont became a state, it was _____.
2. Building material found in Vermont and New Hampshire
4. Important crop in Maine
5. Most New Hampshire citizens' political position
7. Maine's largest city
9. Two-letter abbreviation of the state that once was New York's rival in claiming Vermont
10. Capital of Maine
11. Not as many people work at catching these in Maine as in the past.
16. Two-letter abbreviation of the state that once owned Maine

Acadia National Park, a strip of seacoast and islands in northern Maine

NH *Purple lilac*

ME *White pine cone and tassel*

KILLINGTON MOUNTAIN

VT *Red clover*

Word List

Acadia	Burlington	granite	Montpelier	potato
Augusta	conservative	independent	mountains	ski
Bean	election	lumber	NH	tax
	fish	MA	Portland	

WASHINGTON, DISTRICT OF COLUMBIA

Washington, D.C., is the capital of the United States. The city of Washington is not in a state. It is in a special district called the District of Columbia. This area of land, located between Virginia and Maryland on the bank of the Potomac River, is controlled by Congress. As the capital, Washington, D.C., is a symbol of unity for all the states. It is the center for the nation's government. Today, the District totals about sixty-eight square miles. The Washington metropolitan area is one of the largest urban areas in the nation; it includes suburbs in Virginia as well as those in Maryland extending up to Baltimore.

Washington, D.C., was planned by Congress to be the nation's capital, and Congress decided to name the city after the nation's first president. George Washington never lived there, but he appointed a French architect, Pierre L'Enfant, to design the city. In 1800, the government moved to Washington, and John Adams became the first president to live in the White House. The Capitol, intended to be the meeting place of Congress, was barely finished when the British burned it during the War of 1812. It was promptly rebuilt. Today, most Washingtonians make a living by working for government, providing services, or working in tourism. Young and old alike enjoy the Smithsonian Institution museums and other attractions located along the Mall. Visitors come to Washington all year, but a favorite time is in spring when the famous cherry trees, a gift from Japan, are in bloom around town.

Washington, D.C., was at first entirely controlled by Congress. Citizens now elect their own city council and mayor, but Congress still has the right to regulate the city and its spending. The people of Washington elect a representative to Congress, but that person cannot vote on laws. Even though the city is so important to the nation, poverty and crime have been serious problems there.

Across

1. City where government is, such as Washington, D.C.
7. The Washington _____ is at the far end of the Mall from the Capitol.
9. People who burned the Capitol in the War of 1812
11. Name of the grassy rectangle extending from the Capitol
12. Name of the institution that has many museums in Washington, D.C.
13. Kind of pink blossoms famous in Washington, D.C.
15. Name of the river that borders Washington, D.C.
16. Washington, D.C.'s, only one has no vote in Congress.
17. This president's memorial is at the far end of the Reflecting Pool.

Down

Washington, D.C.

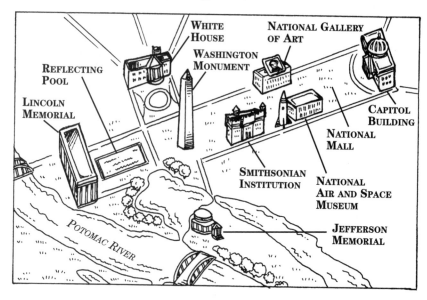

2. Last name of the first president to live in the White House
3. Number of states bordering the District of Columbia
4. Washington is not in a state but in a _____.
5. Most people in Washington, D.C., work in services, tourism, or _____.
6. First name of the president who hired an architect to plan the capital
8. Washington, D.C.'s, suburbs extend in this state all the way to Baltimore.

10. Group finally responsible for city government in Washington, D.C.
13. Building where Congress meets
14. Country that gave cherry trees to Washington, D.C.

Word List

Adams	Capitol	George	Mall	representative
British	cherry	government	Maryland	Smithsonian
capital	Congress	Japan	Monument	two
	district	Lincoln	Potomac	

ANSWERS

Hawaii, pages 6–7

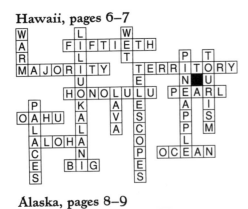

Alaska, pages 8–9

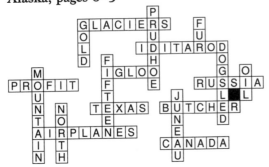

California, pages 10–11

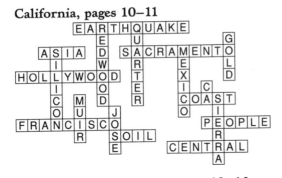

Washington and Oregon, pages 12–13

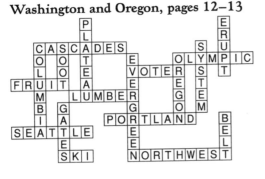

Nevada and Utah, pages 14–15

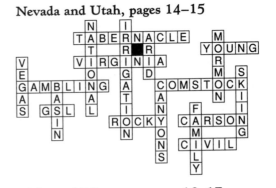

Idaho and Montana, pages 16–17

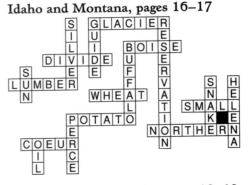

Wyoming and Colorado, pages 18–19

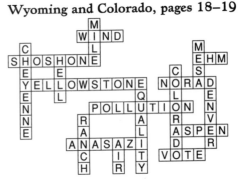

Arizona and New Mexico, pages 20–21

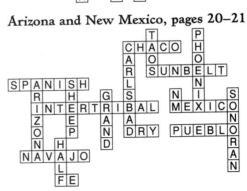

Texas and Oklahoma, pages 22–23

```
    S P A C E        C
    L        S E C O N D
    A        P      W  A
    R E F I N E R I E S  L
  C O      N      N  T  L
  O T      A S T R O D O M E    H
S I X T Y  U      L  E R    A
  T  N     S      E  R  S T A R
  H O U S T O N    T  I
  O        I       O  T
  N        N       P  O C
                      R  I
                      Y  T U
                         O  L
                         R  S
                         Y  A
```

North Dakota and South Dakota, pages 24–25

```
  G O L D     H
  A      H    O
C O R N   M I S S O U R I
  I      M    E     C
  S      E    S T    B L A C K
H O M E S T A K E    I ■ I
  N      A    A      R U S H M O R E
  W O U N D E D       M
         R    S      A
  W H E A T          B  R
              B      A  C
              D A K O T A
                        R
```

Iowa, Kansas, and Nebraska, pages 26–27

```
    L      C
  M I S S O U R I        C O R N
    N      N             E
W I C H I T A     U N I C A M E R A L   B
H E  O     I          R    R    O       L
E    L     N          R    O            E
A    N   N E B R A S K A   L            E
T        N          N      L  R A I L R O A D
    F L A T         C      E            I
    A ■  L          E            H O G S  N
A I R P L A N E                          
    M    E
         Y
```

Minnesota, Wisconsin, and Michigan, pages 28–29

```
  M I C H I G A N     D E T R O I T
  A      E            W       W    W
  D   L  R   F I S H I N G     I    I
  I   A  M       O            C    C
  S   N  A M E R I C A         E    E
  O   N  N       D    C
M O O S E   I    A    H
  N      N  N    N A S S E M B L Y
  J        S          E
C O L L E G E S       L A K E S
  B                        E
  S T
```

Missouri and Arkansas, pages 30–31

```
         W        K C
         E        E
J E F F E R S O N  C L I N T O N
  A    T   H       O      T
  R    O   O       U      R
  M A N U F A C T U R I N G  A
  I    H   S       S      L
H I G H  T I C  P A P E R
  N    T       N      W
    L I T T L E  A    A R K
      T        N      Y
    D I A M O N D S
```

Illinois, pages 32–33

```
    S P R I N G F I E L D   C
    A            I          H
  W I N D       I N S T I T U T E
  S D    B      C          C
  K U    B U L L S   H I   A
  Y U    L      C    I L   G
  S E A R S  E  G  P L A I N S  O H I O
  C R    T   S  I  L    X      H
  R A I R P L A N E  E A S T   A
  A D                         R
  P E                         E
  E
  R
```

Indiana and Ohio, pages 34–35

```
        E A S T
      G  P
I N D I A N A P O L I S    O S U
    G R  A              L  T A
    R Y  L           S  I  A T
        A         G  O  M  T E
        C O L U M B U S  E R I E
        H        A  T  S  O
R       I        C  H     O    S
A C I N C I N N A T I  T H E A T E R S
C   E   N        E  O     R      T
E   O            R  N  O R D I N A N C E
    N            S        N      E
    S A L T               E      L
```

Tennessee, Kentucky, and West Virginia, pages 36–37

```
          C O T T O N     W V
          H        C      O O
      T H O R O U G H B R E D  O
      V    L        L      T
      D A N I E L   M U S I C  O
    L      S        E      R   U
M A N U F A C T U R I N G      R
  K   N    O        R      C   I
  E   I             O  F R A N K F O R T
  S M O K Y         R      S   S
                    N A S H V I L L E
```

Mississippi and Louisiana, pages 38–39

```
      J
    P L A N T A T I O N
    R          U  O
  T R    K     G R A S ■ V
S E R V I C E S  B P E N  K I N G
  H A   N       A E     C
  R D           T N     K
P I N E Y    C O S T U M E S
  M   F      N  I     B
  P   R A N C E I N   G U M B O
      N              R
      C A T C H E Z   G U L F
      E
```

Alabama and Georgia, pages 40–41

```
              A
          P E A N U T S
B U S   O   I   L     M
I   R   R E P R E S E N T A T I O N
R   E   E   D   N      N
M M M   W  M    T      T   F
I O K E F E N O K E E   A  O J R
N B I  H  E V    N      G  R
G I    H  I      B   M  O  E
H A L F      S O U T H E A S T
A E  C O L O N Y     L  R Y
M        D E L T A
```

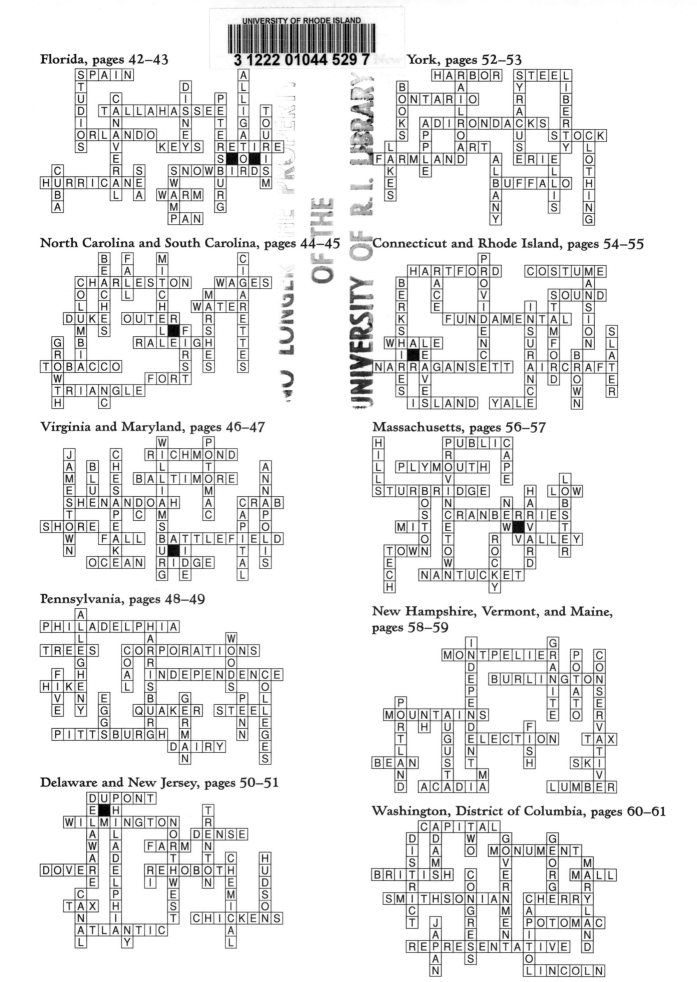

Florida, pages 42–43

New York, pages 52–53

North Carolina and South Carolina, pages 44–45

Connecticut and Rhode Island, pages 54–55

Virginia and Maryland, pages 46–47

Massachusetts, pages 56–57

Pennsylvania, pages 48–49

New Hampshire, Vermont, and Maine, pages 58–59

Delaware and New Jersey, pages 50–51

Washington, District of Columbia, pages 60–61